THE LIGHT OF DAY

THE LIGHT OF DAY

by Graham Swannell

CHAPPELL PLAYS

LONDON

A member of the Chappell and Intersong Music Group

First published 1988 by
Chappell Plays Ltd,
129 Park Street, London W1Y 3FA

ISBN 0 85676 135 4

Typeset and printed by Commercial Colour Press, London E7.
Cover design by Robin Lowry.

THE LIGHT OF DAY was first presented at the Lyric Studio, Hammersmith, on 27 August 1987, with thc following cast:

BEL	Claire Hackett
RALPH	Nigel Terry
LOUISE	Nicola Pagett

Directed by Peter James
Designed by Poppy Mitchell

CHARACTERS

LOUISE	late thirties
RALPH	forty
BEL	twenty

also a man in his early twenties

The play takes place in a room in the Hotel Paradise in Montmartre.

A hot summer. Late afternoon—night—dawn

The *Light of Day* can be performed without an interval, or with an interval after Act One, Scene Two.

Photograph by Sarah Ainslie from the Lyric Theatre, Hammersmith production of The Light of Day.

ACT ONE

Scene One

Sunset

A room in the Hotel Paradise in Montmartre. A glass door with shutters opening on to a balcony. A bed, two armchairs, a dressing table. Two other doors lead from the room, one to the bathroom, the other to the corridor.

The room is strewn with travelling items: a case, newspapers, rock magazines, cassettes, a cassette recorder, clothes, more clothes drying on the balcony, books, empty bottles and a bottle of red wine with two glasses. It is a hot summer night.

LOUISE *stands in the doorway. She is a strikingly attractive professional woman. She is dressed in chic summer clothes. She carries a smart satchel bag which contains: a filofax, business papers, make-up and the bare essentials for a stop-over.*

RALPH *stands holding the door handle. He is also attractive and still retains a boyish charm. He has longish hair and is clean shaven. He is hastily dressed in jeans. When fully dressed he wears an open neck soft white shirt and high heeled leather boots.*

BEL *sits on the bed. A young woman with an innocent face and long hair. She is dressed only in briefs, and she covers her breasts with her hands. When dressed her clothes are late eighties. Doc Martens, ankle socks, short black skirt and loose T-shirt.*

The lights snap on and the TABLEAUX *is held for a considerable time, i.e., twenty seconds.* LOUISE *and* RALPH *eye each other. They are still deeply in love with each other. As the dialogue starts,* BEL *dresses and so eventually does* RALPH.

LOUISE (*angrily*) Well. Hello.

RALPH (*cheerfully*) Louise.

LOUISE Hello, Ralph.

RALPH Hello. You've cut your hair.

LOUISE I know.

RALPH Listen, huh, listen, I know, I know what you are thinking.

LOUISE You do?

RALPH Oh yes, I know, but it's not, it's not what you think.

LOUISE It's not?

RALPH Oh, no. No. I mean, I haven't even got a pack.

LOUISE You haven't?

RALPH No.

BEL Oh, I have.

RALPH What?

BEL I have a pack. (*She produces a pack of condoms.*)

(*Pause.*)

LOUISE (*sardonically*) It's always the women who pick up the tab.

RALPH What? Now listen to me Louise, before you start up, there's a few points I'd like to make.

BEL Louise? Louise who?

RALPH (*matter of fact*) Oh, that's Louise.

LOUISE Hello.

RALPH My wife.

BEL Your wife?

LOUISE My husband.

BEL Oh no!

RALPH (*expansively*) So you managed to find me all right.

LOUISE (*bitterly*) Oh, I thought you might be here.

BEL (*shocked, hurt*) You're not, are you? You're not *married*, are you?

LOUISE Seventeen years.

RALPH Seventeen years? Never.

LOUISE Eighteen in September.

RALPH No, it can't be. Eighteen years?

LOUISE Parliament Hill Fields. 1969. The Pink Floyd.

BEL (*scornfully*) The Pink Floyd.

LOUISE How could you forget?

RALPH Well. Well. It's a...

LOUISE Long time?

(*Pause.* RALPH *dresses.*)

BEL I don't believe it. You. I thought. (*Determinedly*) Look, excuse me.

LOUISE Yes?

BEL I'm sorry. I didn't know. I really had no idea he was married.

LOUISE You didn't guess?

BEL No, I didn't and anyway, he never told me. If I'd known...

LOUISE Would it have made any difference?

BEL (*indignantly*) Of course it would. I wouldn't have let myself. I wouldn't have.

RALPH What are you talking about? You don't have to justify anything to Louise.

BEL Yes, I do. I want her to know. (*Angrily*) This is absolutely not my scene. Well, it's not! Look, I don't even like married men.

LOUISE You don't like married men?

BEL Of course not. They're...well...they're...

LOUISE They're what?

BEL You know.

RALPH What is she talking about?

BEL Oh, you know. Well, you know, don't you?

LOUISE Yes, I think I know.

BEL Anyway, they never change their underpants.

RALPH What did she say?

LOUISE Oh, I'm sure she didn't mean you.

BEL They're all so deceitful. They're always looking out for their next wife.

RALPH (*incredulously*) What? Looking out for their next wife!

BEL Well, they are, aren't they?

LOUISE I don't know. Are you?

RALPH Who, me? Looking for another wife? Me?

(*Slight pause.*)

BEL (*genuinely*) I really am sorry. I wouldn't be in this position if he hadn't lied to me.

LOUISE Oh, he lied.

BEL I find all this extremely embarrassing.

RALPH I did not lie. I never lied to you.

BEL I hate being put in this position. I feel so *DIRTY*.

RALPH (*angrily*) I did not lie. Christ Almighty!

LOUISE All right, Ralph.

RALPH Well!

BEL (*abruptly*) You do believe me, don't you? I feel terrible. You do believe me? I'm sorry. I didn't know!

RALPH Oh, for God's sake, shut up!

LOUISE (*emphatically*) All right, it's OK! Really, it's OK!

BEL (*brief pause*) It's OK?

LOUISE Yes. It's OK.

(*Pause*)

BEL Oh, thank you. Thank you. (*Brief pause*) Oh, good. (*Brief pause*) You know, I thought you looked a nice person.

RALPH (*shocked*) Nice person? Dear God! I see, all the conspirators.

BEL I should have known better. All that talk. I thought. . . Oh, but you're all the same. A lovely wife at home and you're still not satisfied.

RALPH A lovely wife *at home*?

BEL You could have told me. I mean, what are you up to?

RALPH I think you're talking to the wrong person. You should be asking my lovely wife.

LOUISE Me? I'm not up to anything.

RALPH Oh come on Louise, it's too late to act the innocent with me.

LOUISE But *I* haven't done anything.

RALPH Listen, in the first place, I may be married but I'm very particular about personal hygiene. I believe standards of decency are absolutely indispensable. In the second place I did not lie to her. She never asked if I was married and I never felt the need to mention it. If failing to tell her constitutes a lie, let him without sin cast the first stone. You know what I mean? Well, you know, don't you?

LOUISE Me? No, I don't know.

RALPH Well, you should.

LOUISE Why?

RALPH (*hesitates*) Have you no idea why I took off? Why I'm here?

LOUISE No, it's a complete mystery. Why are you here?

RALPH (*triumphantly*) Well, it's very simple. (*To* BEL) I saw her. I saw you.

LOUISE Saw me what?

RALPH I was at the bedroom window. I was behind the curtain.

LOUISE (*amused*) Behind the curtain? What were you doing behind the curtain?

RALPH Christ! I saw you with Paul.

LOUISE Paul?

RALPH (*exasperated*) I was at the window. I saw both of you. He had his hand up your skirt!

LOUISE (*nonchalantly*) Hand up my skirt?

RALPH Yes. He was all over you.

LOUISE No, you're mistaken. . . we were looking for my purse.

RALPH (*outraged*) Looking for your *purse*?

LOUISE We had to pay the taxi.

RALPH What are you talking about? He brought you home in his car.

LOUISE Actually it's a company car.

RALPH All right, company car! But he certainly wasn't looking for your *purse*.

LOUISE (*abruptly, moving to* BEL) You see. . . Oh by the way, what's your name?

BEL Bel.

LOUISE You see Bel, we'd had this meeting. We were discussing next months' issue. We were discussing whether to do a piece on new women designers. It went on till late. Unfortunately there was a lot of drink about and well. . . Paul's an old friend, and a colleague.

RALPH A colleague? Working late with a colleague? What kind of excuse is that?

LOUISE You mean to say, I'm not permitted to embrace a close friend? To say goodnight?

RALPH (*decisively*) That's exactly what I mean. I'm not hanging around at home while you're out embracing *close friends*. What do you think that makes me?

LOUISE I don't know.

BEL What can you do?

LOUISE I know.

RALPH (*to* BEL) Listen, I'm not talking about a goodnight peck. Social graces. No, I'm talking about *deep contact*. (*To* LOUISE) Consenting, intimate, and it didn't look like it was the first time either.

LOUISE I don't know how you have the nerve! It's a pack of lies! It's a pathetic excuse to justify this, THIS. (*Pointing at the bed*) Anyway it was the dead of night. I don't see how you could have seen. It was pitch black out there.

(*Slight pause.*)

RALPH You left the car door open.

LOUISE What?

RALPH You forgot about the inside light.

LOUISE It wasn't. . .it wasn't on, was it?

RALPH Oh yes, a bright yellow light.

LOUISE (*brief pause*) Ah. Damn.

RALPH (*expansively to* BEL) You see. You see!

LOUISE (*recovering quickly*) Yes. Well. I must say, in my defence, it was a warm night.

RALPH That's a defence?

LOUISE (*bitterly*) Like tonight? (*Brief pause*) I'd had too much white wine.

RALPH Oh come on Louise, no one gets drunk on white wine.

LOUISE Well, you might not, but I do.

BEL So do I.

LOUISE It's just a fact, Ralph. You can't ignore facts.

RALPH (*with emphasis*) That't what I thought.

(*Slight pause.*)

LOUISE Yes, but that's no reason for you to take off.

RALPH Oh, isn't it?

LOUISE (*honestly*) We did nothing. Nothing.

(*Pause.*)

I don't suppose I could have a drink?

BEL Sure.

(BEL *pours two glasses of wine and gives one to* LOUISE. LOUISE *drinks.*)

(*Pause.*)

(*cheerfully*) For what it's worth, all this makes me feel a lot. . . well it's nice to know I'm not the only. . . happy days. (BEL *drinks.*) I tell you what, I think you should have knocked first.

LOUISE It's more fun if you don't knock.

BEL Yes, but you could have been anyone.

LOUISE Well, I'm not anyone. (*To* RALPH) Am I?

RALPH You have to understand that Louise doesn't recognize the rules anymore.

BEL I'm sorry, what rules?

RALPH You know, the rules.

LOUISE He means, his rules.

RALPH No, I do not! You know bloody well what rules I'm talking about!

(RALPH *exits into the bathroom to get a glass.*)

(*A* YOUNG MAN *pushes open the door that has been left slightly ajar. He steps into the room and eyes the two ladies.*)

MAN (*salaciously*) Bonsoir, Mesdames.

BEL (*giggles*) Bonsoir, bonsoir.

(*The* YOUNG MAN *blows her a kiss and then hearing* RALPH *in the bathroom exits.* RALPH *enters.*)

RALPH Who was that?

LOUISE I don't know.

RALPH (*shutting the door*) It wasn't Paul, was it?

LOUISE Paul? Here? Oh no, Paul's much more...anyway he can't speak French.

RALPH No, he can't do anything, except stick his...

(RALPH *pours a drink.*)

Working late with a colleague! Do me a favour, that's my line. (*Brief pause*) Hell, it's hot.

(*Pause.* RALPH *goes out on to the balcony.*)

BEL (*tentatively*) I love heat, don't you?

LOUISE Mmnn.

RALPH (*vindictively*) You should have been in Madrid.

LOUISE Madrid?

BEL (*innocently*) It's where we met. We came up last weekend.

(*Pause.*)

LOUISE I see. And how was Madrid?

RALPH Madrid was a *furnace.*

BEL Yes, it was really steamy.

LOUISE (*hurt*) Really.

RALPH It was even hotter than that night here.

BEL Oh. You've been to the Hotel Paradise before?

(*Silence.*)

(*embarrassed*) How's England?

LOUISE England? England's OK. It was raining when I left.

BEL I hate rain, don't you?

LOUISE No, I rather like rain. It's good for the garden. (*To* RALPH) The roses are doing fine, if you're interested. Still I had a pleasant trip here. I travelled light this time. I didn't want the bother of cases.

BEL Who needs cases?

LOUISE I wanted to be free of all that.

BEL Did you fly?

LOUISE (*to* RALPH) No, I did the old-fashioned thing and caught the ferry. The sun came out while we were crossing, but it was quite windy.

BEL I don't like the wind. It makes me feel strange.

LOUISE I'm not terribly fond of lightning.

BEL Hail is another.

(RALPH *enters from the balcony.*)

RALPH (*impatiently*) Well, we had a bloody awful journey here. Bloody awful. We were stuck in a carriage full of migrant workers. This guy drank beer. He stank out the compartment. And there were his kids, crying and staring at me, and picking their noses. I tell you, it was bloody awful.

LOUISE It sounds like hell.

RALPH Well it was, bloody hell.

BEL I slept of course. I don't know why, but I seem to be able to sleep anywhere.

LOUISE It's a gift.

(*Brief pause.*)

RALPH One of the migrants. The drinker. He had this Lee Van Cleef way of looking at you, and he didn't take to me at all. He thought I was looking at his missus. His senorita. He thought I actually fancied her.

LOUISE And did you?

RALPH Of course I didn't. On the contrary, I was just idly looking in her direction while having a think. A good think about things. About the state of play. If I'd told him what was in my head, I think he might have cheered. He must have had at least six kids.

LOUISE Why would he have cheered?

RALPH God knows.

(*Silence.* RALPH *pours a drink. He drinks.*)

BEL What do you think of the room? It's good, isn't it? It's got a great view. You can see the whole city from up here. Notre Dame. The Left Bank.

RALPH Who do you think you're talking to? You think she doesn't know? You think she hasn't seen the view? Of course she's seen the view. She's seen all the views. Haven't you?

(*Slight pause.*)

BEL I'm sorry. Would anyone like a crisp?

LOUISE No thank you.

BEL I love crisps. (*She eats.*) I'm quite hungry. If you gave me the money I'd go and get something to eat.

RALPH (*abruptly*) I'll tell you what I thought as I gazed at that senorita. I thought. What a potful of piss we have to take from women these days.

LOUISE I beg your pardon?

RALPH (*emotionally*) Oh, don't deny it. You were with another man. It was the *last straw*. There I am at home. Waiting. Thinking you're working. When all the time you're with another man. I just had to take off. I had to get out. You looked so...

LOUISE What? What did I look?

RALPH Happy.

BEL (*brief pause*) Does anyone fancy something to eat?

RALPH I don't care when men look at you. I just care when you look back.

LOUISE I felt the need for some attention. What attention do I get from you? Ever since I started to work, ever since I've had a separate life, a life that does not *entirely* revolve around you...

RALPH I don't need this.

LOUISE I know you don't like it.

RALPH I don't need to take it.

LOUISE (*vehemently*) You hate me working. You hate me having a successful job. It would be all right if I worked in a shop!

RALPH Oh God, why did you come! It certainly wasn't to see me. I mean, is something wrong? It's not Jordan, is it?

LOUISE (*implacable*) No. Jordan's fine.

RALPH Are you sure?

LOUISE What do you think?

RALPH She's been asking about me?

LOUISE Of course.

RALPH Oh, Hell. What did you say?

LOUISE Look, Jordan is in good health, believe me. I just told her it was *time*.

RALPH (*exasperated*) *Time?* Time for what?

BEL (*hastily*) Look, excuse me. I think it would be a good idea if we all went out to eat. You can't fight on an empty stomach. (*To* RALPH) Do you want to eat?

RALPH Eat?

BEL We could go to Chartiers.

RALPH Do I look as if I want to eat?

BEL Well, I can't eat on my own. (*She sits on bed.*) I'd settle for a cheeseburger the way I feel.

(RALPH *pours a drink. Pause.*)

LOUISE God, it's hot.

(LOUISE *goes out on to the balcony.* BEL *looks at* RALPH *and* LOUISE.)

BEL Well, I've never wanted to be married. It's never appealed to me. I couldn't bear someone in my space all the time. Having to explain yourself, your every move. That kind of thing gives me the creeps.

RALPH You should have been a pop star.

BEL Me, a pop singer?

RALPH You've an unlimited capacity for talking crap.

LOUISE Ralph.

RALPH What does she know about marriage?

BEL When I was younger I always wanted to be married. That was until I learnt men never tell the truth.

RALPH Oh no.

BEL It's true. You'd say anything. Men never tell you what they're really thinking. The only way you know what they think is by looking at their eyes, and their eyes are usually looking down your dress.

RALPH Oh, do we have to?

BEL Well, a girlfriend of mine did it in an alleyway.

RALPH What did she say?

BEL Up against a wet wall. Against a tree. She was hoping for a white wedding. She did it standing up.

RALPH Standing up? No one does it standing up!

LOUISE Oh, shut up, Ralph.

RALPH (*shocked*) I don't understand. I don't understand how you can come in here and take her side.

LOUISE I'm not taking sides.

RALPH Yes, you are. You think I'm not aware? It's happening all the time. You're all taking sides. It makes me feel very . . .

LOUISE OK! OK. . .let's get this over with!

RALPH Well!

LOUISE Come on, come on, spit it out. Let's have the *BIG SPIT*.

RALPH Well, look at you. In your Bond Street clothes. You *never* dressed like that before. You never felt part of *that life*. That life was for other people you had no respect for whatsoever. What's happened to you? And your hair?

LOUISE You don't like it?

RALPH What is it? The executive cut?

LOUISE I thought you might like it.

BEL I like it. It's neat. I was thinking of getting my hair cut, but I don't know, it's. . .

RALPH A big decision?

BEL It can be, a change of style.

RALPH What is it with you women? What is this hair business? This make-up? You never used to wear it, not in the old days.

LOUISE I'm getting older, Ralph.

RALPH Yes, but what is make-up? Powder your face. Lipstick. What's it all about? I don't know. I mean, I do know, but you tell me.

LOUISE (*calmly*) When I look good, I feel good.

BEL We all feel good.

RALPH (*decisively*) No, you wear it because you still want *men* to want you. You want *Paul* to want you. Oh, you come on with the equal this, equal that crap, but all the time you're damned if you're going to give up the old tricks. You know, 'the old tricks'. (*Brief pause, to* BEL) You probably think this doesn't matter, but I tell you it does matter. And the only reason they're looking down your dress darlin', is because it's low enough to look down.

(*Pause.*)

LOUISE Is that it?

BEL It looks like it.

LOUISE So you don't think I have a right to do what I like.

RALPH Is that what you call it?

LOUISE (*violently*) My God Ralph, I have a right! (*Brief pause, calmly*) I can do as I please. There's no question about it.

BEL Where has he been the last fifteen years?

LOUISE God knows.

RALPH (*emphatically*) I'm telling you, you can't do as you please with me.

LOUISE I can appreciate all this must be extremely difficult for you. I know you'd like to continue to run my life.

RALPH What?

LOUISE I don't think we're talking about anything else.

RALPH Listen, it's all or nothing with me. If you are going to love, it's all the way. I'm not afraid of that. I'm not keeping back a separate part. A secret part. I'm not afraid of you knowing all there is to know about me.

BEL He's some kind of jealous guy, isn't he?

LOUISE Is he?

BEL I think he should be telling all this to his mother.

RALPH What?

LOUISE (*abruptly*) Look Ralph, I dropped everything. I couldn't stand it after a few days. I had to come. Doesn't that mean anything to you? Well?

(*Pause.* LOUISE *takes her filofax from her bag and flicks through it.*)

LOUISE How long are we staying?

RALPH *We*?

LOUISE I ought to phone through in the morning. I must be back by Monday. I think it's best if we fly back tomorrow. I've got some important...

RALPH Meetings? We all know about meetings.

LOUISE I have to work.

RALPH So do I.

LOUISE I'm responsible for my staff.

RALPH Good God, you used to let your hair down once!

LOUISE Yes, when it was long.

RALPH No. You used to let it all go. (*To* BEL) She didn't always used to work. She only works now because that's what she wants. I mean, we don't need the money. Oh no, she didn't want to work before, she just hung out. She hung out at home. It didn't seem to bother her at all. *I've* always had to work. Someone had to. Someone had to sweat, to sell themselves. Freelance this, cover that Band, sit through that gig, deadlines, blah, blah, blah. And all for what? To come home to an Indian take-away, when you knew damn well I hated Indian food.

BEL You don't like Indian? I love it. I could do with a curry right now.

LOUISE It was a mistake.

RALPH Rubbish.

LOUISE I forgot.

RALPH You didn't forget. You never forget.

LOUISE How can you say that? After all I've done. After all those years of looking after Jordan. After all those meals. All those bloody meals. Racking my brains each day to produce a meal so we'd all have something decent inside us. None of it rubbish. No chemical rubbish. (*To* BEL) You've no idea how *boring* it can be. Each morning, the same old question, what are we going to eat today? Day in, day out, until in the end I couldn't think about food without screaming! (*Brief pause, with relish*) I wanted. I wanted a taste of the life *you've had* ever since you can remember. Dear God, I can't tell you how good it feels, to get into my car, push in a cassette, turn up the music, and drive off to work. It's bliss. Bliss.

(*Pause.*)

RALPH (*shakes his head*) We used to have such a good life.

LOUISE Oh come on, it can still be good.

RALPH No, it's gone.

LOUISE (*sighs*) Gone?

RALPH I can't see it any more. I hardly see you anymore. You've replaced me with a life style I have no wish to live.

LOUISE But Ralph, I don't possess you. You're free to do what you like. I've no wish to possess you, and I don't see why you should have to possess me. If only you could accept that.

RALPH No, that's not it. It's just I have this feeling I'm being used by you. I can't shake it. You're just using me to make up your pretty picture. To round out your life.

LOUISE You, of course, don't use me.

RALPH No.

LOUISE (*sarcastically*) No?

RALPH No, I've never used you. That's not the way I see it at all.

LOUISE Well, I have to tell you, I'm not prepared to sacrifice what I've achieved. It's you. You've got to do it. You've got to find a new way of seeing me. A new way of seeing our life. Ralph? Where are you going? (RALPH *exits.*) Ralph? (*Silence.* LOUISE *lights a cigarette.*) Cigarette?

BEL No thanks, I don't. (*Pause*) Huh.

LOUISE What?

BEL It's pot luck with men.

LOUISE Is it?

BEL Well, you never know.

LOUISE No, you never know.

(*Pause.*)

BEL There are some men you see at a party, at a gathering, hanging out somewhere, and you know, you have a good look, don't you? You give them a good going over.

LOUISE Do you?

BEL Yes. The way they stand. Their hair. Their general state. And if it's all right, if it's clean, if it's tasty, well, you think, I wouldn't mind a piece of that, you know, given the right situation, the right time. You think, I'll have that. I'll have it.

LOUISE And you did.

BEL Oh come on, you know I didn't know about you.

LOUISE You didn't?

BEL No. I really meant what I said. I don't lie. That's not my style. (*Brief pause*) Anyway it all depends. Finally, when all is said and done, it all depends on what you have to put up with when he opens his mouth. When the words start.

LOUISE The words?

BEL When he starts to drone on about his life. They're always wittering on about the meaning of their lives. God knows why, it's as clear as day to me.

LOUISE You don't like to talk about life?

BEL It's a joke. And the joke is, while he's trying to impress me with his philosophical themes, all I'm thinking is can he get it up? And when it's up, will it stay up? Will it stay up long enough to make it worth my while? Am I right? Of course I'm right. You see, *I take it as I see it.* (*Brief pause*) Mind you, I can put up with an amazing amount of chat if he's got a nice tight arse.

LOUISE And *love*?

BEL Love? I didn't think we were talking about love.

LOUISE No. (*Pause*) My daughter, my daughter Jordan, when she was about five, she said to me, she said, life began with a Dinosaur egg and in that egg was a man. (BEL *laughs*) Oh, there's no wine left. (*Brief pause*) Yes, it's changing opinions that is so difficult. They're so deep. You can't dig them out. It takes too long. More than my lifetime, and my life's half gone already. I can't waste any more time. You see, I left school early. I went to work on the *Evening News*, but I wasn't particularly happy. I mean, I'd always been interested in art, although I never painted much. I would have but I didn't have the space. I had this small room in Kilburn. There was this sky-light and that was all the natural light I had. And in the summer it was unbearable. The heat in the roof. I never used the gas ring. I just had salads, tuna fish, that kind of thing. Well, finally I applied to Wimbledon Art College and was accepted. That's where I met Ralph. He lived in Hammersmith. We used to walk by the river and drink in the Dove. Do you know the Dove?

BEL No.

LOUISE Well, one day, Ralph was talking about buying a motorbike and I said, We'll have to have a sidecar for the baby. I wasn't pregnant. It just seemed so logical. So I never finished college.

(*Pause.* RALPH *bursts into the room clutching a bottle of wine.*)

RALPH Argh!

LOUISE Ralph? What is it? Ralph?

RALPH Before. In the old days. We were never against each other. We weren't separate. We were one. We were the vanguard. Rock and Roll. A new kind of life. Where the hell has it *gone*? All I see now. . . is self-obsession. That's *all* I see. Self-obsession!

LOUISE (*incredulously*) And it wasn't before?

RALPH Before? Before it was innocent. It was so easy. You fancied a session and you had it. It was easy. Plentiful. A rich harvest. In the old days you could fuck without any back chat whatsoever!

(*Blackout.*)

Scene Two

Night

LOUISE *is outside on the balcony.*

RALPH *is sitting in an armchair. He has a glass of wine in his hand. The bottle is three-quarters empty.*

BEL *is curled up on the bed.*

The sound of the occasional car. The last chords of a piece of jazz from another room.

LOUISE *lights a cigarette.* RALPH *laughs and drinks.*

RALPH *You* talk about seeing. Well, *I* see it. I could see it on that train, but now I can really see it. I tell you, there's no other way out of this Louise.

LOUISE Mmnn? (*She enters*) What did you say?

RALPH You listen to this. Ha! You see, there was this man in his car at the lights. He was stuck at the lights.

LOUISE What man?

RALPH Oh, just a man. He was waiting at the lights, when this woman walks by.

LOUISE What woman?

LOUISE Oh come on Louise, any old woman. You know, small tits, OK arse.

LOUISE That's not any woman.

RALPH Well, I've settled for a lot worse in my time. We all have. Huh. No, the point is you have to bear in mind she's not exceptional. She's not rough, but she certainly isn't quality. I suppose one might call her average. Anyway, what do you think the man in the car does?

LOUISE Oh, whistles?

RALPH No.

LOUISE Calls out to her?

RALPH Yes. He winds down his window and hangs out, and shouts, Fancy a ride darlin'? Fancy a leg over?

LOUISE Oh, God.

RALPH I know. Talk about style.

LOUISE Typical.

RALPH Well, that's debatable, but actually that's my point. You see, a woman sways past, any woman, a complete stranger, and this man, this man is virtually whipping it out. Huh! Well, eventually the lights change. Up comes the old green light and off he blasts. Straight through the gears, smoking exhaust, the works. It's all to impress her, of course.

LOUISE (*mocks*) Really?

RALPH Yes, don't I look clever? Don't I look smart. That kind of thing. Well, to cut it short, he didn't score. Huh. No, he certainly didn't score. He just, well, he just fucked his gears.

BEL Prat.

RALPH I couldn't agree more. (*Drinks*) So on I trot. It's a pleasant day. The sun is high. There's a lot of flesh about. A lot of loose summer T-shirts. How I like it. How we all like it. God bless summer, that's what I say. Or used to say. When this memory surfaces. I get this flashback. I'm standing at that coffee bar next to platform 19 on Waterloo station. There I am trying to put off the first cigarette of the day...

BEL You don't smoke.

RALPH That's right. I've beat it since, but that morning I'd failed. There I am, when this woman...

LOUISE Oh no, not another woman.

RALPH Oh yes, yes, another woman. She approaches me, and asks me where I bought these boots. You see, she has a man with her, and it's the man who wants to know, but he hasn't got the nerve to ask, so he gets his lady to do it for him. Well, I mumble some name. While all the time. All the time I'm staring at her face. I'm inhaling the scent of her newly washed hair. I immediately want to lose myself in her.

LOUISE What do you mean?

RALPH (*sincerely*) I told you. I'm not holding anything back.

LOUISE Who is this woman?

RALPH I don't know. I told her the name of the shop and she was gone.

LOUISE What a shame.

RALPH No. That's not my point. You see, it occurred to me as I walked along, that there was a link between the man in the car and myself. I could see that there was very little difference between us. I mean, we both saw a woman, and we both wanted her.

BEL So what else is new?

RALPH What else is new? I tell you, for me, that was new. I had no idea I was like that other man. I thought I was more than that. More than a compulsive... You see, you've no idea what hold you have over us. At that moment of impact, all reason, all dignity, all poise, Gone! GONE! Out the window! Hell. (*Pause*) Well. All this brings me back to the train from Madrid. There I am, sitting on the train, thinking about the whys and wherefores. How you women have gone and shifted the goalposts. When I realize, all my problems... well, I wouldn't have to put up with any of this bother I have here tonight, any of this heartache. I wouldn't have to put up with it if I wasn't so completely at the mercy of my *genitals*. (LOUISE *laughs*) You can laugh. I'm very serious.

LOUISE Genitals?

RALPH If I could resist...

LOUISE Your genitals?

RALPH That's right Louise, my balls and...

LOUISE All right Ralph, I know what genitals are.

RALPH Yes. I'm sure you do. (RALPH *pours a drink. He drinks.*) Well? What do you think? You see what I'm getting at. There's a solution here.

LOUISE Solution? What solution?

RALPH If you can't compromise the way you use to. If you can't appreciate my point of view. All I say is, not any more. *NOT ANY MORE!*

LOUISE Not any more what?

RALPH I don't know why I didn't see it years ago.

LOUISE Do you know what he's talking about?

BEL I haven't a clue.

RALPH (*triumphantly*) I am out. Out! I'm off out from under. I'm no domestic. Chew your balls off. I'm no bloody hat rack. I'm finished with all this stuff!

LOUISE It's the heat.

BEL It must be.

LOUISE Or the wine.

RALPH (*impatiently*) Don't you understand what I'm saying? I'm saying I'm finished with sex. I've had it with sex!

LOUISE (*incredilously*) Sex! You've had it with sex? *You*? Huh! Since when? Huh. I mean, since when have you finished with sex?

RALPH Since when?

LOUISE Yes, since when?

RALPH Since about an hour ago.

LOUISE An hour ago?

RALPH Yes.

LOUISE What, a whole hour? Sixty minutes? How have you managed it?

RALPH (*humourless*) The first hour's easy.

LOUISE (*affectionately*) Oh Ralph, Ralph, what are you talking about? You don't expect me to take this...

RALPH (*vehemently*) No! No! I've seen the light Louise. I'm not going to perish. You can change all the rules but I'm not going under. This is all that's left to me. *Celibacy*.

(*Pause*.)

LOUISE Right. Right. I understand. I do. Huh. I thought for a moment you were talking about something serious.

RALPH (*joyfully*) You can chop off my chopper for all I care. It's useless. It serves no purpose.

BEL Yes, but you've still got to pee.

RALPH I'm speaking symbolically, you idiot!

LOUISE (*hesitates, hurt*) Celibate?

RALPH That's the picture. No pussy, no problems.

(*Pause.*)

LOUISE Oh, this is ridiculous Ralph. This is no answer. Anyway it's impossible, I know you.

RALPH Huh. The trouble I've got into because of this THING between my legs.

LOUISE Well. I don't know what to say. I mean, are you sure you're all right?

RALPH Hey, what is this? Don't you touch me!

LOUISE But Ralph, are you sure? Are you sure you're OK?

RALPH OK? Do I look OK?

LOUISE Well...

RALPH (*patronisingly*) Of course I'm not OK.

LOUISE I didn't think you were.

RALPH I'm completely fucked!

LOUISE That's what I thought.

RALPH You're looking at a guy who totally refuses to be *pussywhipped* for the rest of his life.

(*Brief Pause.*)

LOUISE Well. I think this calls for another drink. (LOUISE *pours a drink. She drinks.*) Pussywhipped.

RALPH You've NO idea what I'm talking about.

LOUISE Yes, but you can't really be serious.

RALPH You think I want this, do you? This is as serious as I can get. This is out over the ledge and nearly gone serious.

BEL Oh come on Louise. Celibate! It's so of the moment, isn't it?

LOUISE Well, sure. I mean, I can understand if people don't want to die. That's simple. But somehow I don't think that's what Ralph's talking about. (*Mockingly*) Actually, I don't think I've ever met a celibate before.

RALPH You don't need to tell us. We all know *that*.

LOUISE Yes, but how does it feel? Is it different? I can appreciate you've only been one for an hour, but give us an insight. Does it make you feel lightheaded or what?

RALPH (*suddenly furious*) Don't you understand? I'm suffering from some kind of disease. I'm ill. *Ill*.

LOUISE (*nonchalantly*) Well, you don't look ill.

BEL No, you don't. You look...

LOUISE In the pink.

RALPH (*stupefied*) In the pink?

LOUISE Mmnn.

RALPH (*suddenly weary, despairingly*) But I don't feel in the pink. It's not normal. This hold. This sex.

(*Brief pause.*)

BEL Well, it has been going on for thousands of years, you know.

RALPH So?

BEL So.

RALPH So? So? So?

BEL So that's a lot of years.

RALPH (*wearily*) Oh God, is that all you've got to say?

BEL (*fiery*) Oh, you want more? Well, I can give you more. I can give you, I've never heard such garbage in all my life! I ask you, what a response. All because you can't get your own way. Spoilt. That's what I call it!

LOUISE Bel.

RALPH (*to himself*) I tell you, I've had enough of her. I really have. (*He lies on the bed.*)

BEL (*with exaggerated enthusiasm*) Well, If I had *any* money I'd go to Florence. If you gave me money I'd go. Florence is beautiful. It's a beautiful place. It makes you feel good.

(*Silence.*)

LOUISE You know, he made me breakfast that morning. I should have known. You hardly ever make me breakfast.

RALPH (*grudgingly*) I make coffee.

BEL I like tea in the morning.

RALPH Then make tea.

LOUISE (*to* BEL) He brought me up this breakfast on a tray. There were the letters and the paper, and there was a cloth on the tray. A yogurt, a boiled egg and a roll.

RALPH A warm roll.

LOUISE Was it warm?

RALPH Of course it was warm. You didn't even notice.

LOUISE Then while I was away at the office that day, he packed his case and left. He didn't even leave a note.

BEL No note?

LOUISE He didn't even leave a drop of milk for my tea when I got back.

BEL That was cruel.

LOUISE As you can imagine, we've been locked together for years, so I worry. I mean, where has he gone? Has he had a remission? Is he wandering about Europe *again* with his pupils the size of a pin head? I mean, I do worry. I get people out looking really quick.

RALPH The bloodhounds.

LOUISE We make phone calls. Dublin. Newcastle. That place in Brussels. Paris. International phone calls. International conversations in various languages. We make a big effort! And all for what? I come all the way here. I cross the water. I come all the way, just to hear him say, he doesn't want to get laid. I ask you.

BEL He should be so lucky. You haven't got the Crown Jewels in there, you know.

RALPH (*dismissive*) Oh shut up, will you.

BEL What does he think we'll do? Burst into tears?

RALPH (*decisively, leaping up, triumphantly*) Shut up. Shut up. You're talking to the wrong man. This is *Liberation Day!* I've finished with your tribe. If it wasn't for the sex I'd have finished years ago. I mean, let's be frank. *Men don't really like women.* If it wasn't for the sex. I mean, do you think we're interested in anything else? In you? In women as women? Interested in what you have to say? Your opinions? Huh! Do you think we listen? Show me a man who listens and I'll show you a freak. A circus act. A salesman. And you know why, don't you? Don't you? Well, I'll tell you.

LOUISE I had a feeling you might.

RALPH Well, look at you. Look at the way you're looking at me. You're so damn superior. You're so obviously right about everything.

BEL (*cheeky*) That's because we are.

RALPH I'll disregard that. (*Anguished.*) How can you expect any other response from me Louise? You dismiss what I say, and you look at me, while I'm saying it, as if I'm something worse than a tin of cat meat.

LOUISE Oh that's not true. You know it isn't. Come on Ralph!

BEL Surely he means, dog meat?

RALPH (*suddenly violent*) Another bloody word from you and I'll rip your tongue out and eat it!

LOUISE (*shocked*) Ralph! Ralph! What's happening to you!

(*Brief pause.*)

What's happened Ralph?

(*Pause.*)

RALPH (*calmer, coldly*) It's all our own fault. We've brought this on ourselves. I mean, we'd say anything for it. That's been our big mistake. We'd say anything we think you want to hear. Lie to ourselves. Lie to you. Thinking it's so special. Thinking you're so special. It's our fault. *Because you're not special.* You woman. You women are just as big a bunch of *bastards* as men. Except. You won't admit it. You can't admit it. You see, we think we're superior, but you *know* you're superior. I mean, if we're not honest with each other, we haven't got a chance. We haven't got a hope.

(*Pause.*)

BEL (*reflects*) You can't have it all neat. You want all the records to be records, and not records and tapes and a few compact discs.

(*Pause.*)

LOUISE (*affectionately*) Oh, Ralph. Ralph. This is Paris. Paris. We're in *Paris*. The City of Lights. The Ile de la Cité. The Boulevard du Montparnasse.

RALPH So?

LOUISE Don't you remember? The Clôserie des Lilas. That time in the Luxembourg Gardens. Why spoil it? (*Pausing, reflects.*) That journey to Chartres. That tiny Vietnamese woman lighting a candle. (*Tenderly.*) That was love. You can't dismiss it. The Place de la Contrescarpe. You can't just call that *sex*.

(*Pause.*)

LOUISE That's not the way I see it. Just because certain influential *men* told us the world was absurd, that life was without meaning, and that love was transitory, it doesn't mean you have to believe it. Maybe it was for them. Maybe they found love hard, and it is hard. Maybe they found it too complicated to fit into their calm, cool theories, and so they dismissed it. But I can't. I believe in love. I have to believe in something, anyway I do. And it's interesting that very few wrote about love. They couldn't. If they did, they would've had to admit there was something more powerful than their bitterness. *Their boring old bitterness.* (*Brief pause*) Oh, don't be bitter Ralph. Nothing grows from it. You'll just poison yourself.

(*Pause.*)

RALPH (*declamatorily*) I was fashioned by a woman.

BEL Oh God, please spare us. Do we have to? Don't tell us how hard it is to be a man. And what a terrible state, the human condition, and how we all end up as a pile of dust, and why are we here, and who are we, and what's it all about. I mean, spare us.

RALPH Answer me one question. *Who* was filling my head when I was a kid? When my father was at work, who was working on me? Who's slapping my legs? Who's taking down my pants and striking me? Then who's telling me not to cry? Who's urging me to play the brave little man? And whose image of that brave little man was it? I mean, what substitute was I? Who said when the cuddling should stop? Who kicked me out of their bed? *Who*?

BEL You're obsessed with sex.

RALPH What do you expect? I'm a man of my time.

BEL (*to* LOUISE) A lot has happened, but nothing, absolutely nothing has changed.

LOUISE (*to* BEL) I agree. I suppose the only significant change that's happened in my lifetime is men now wear earrings.

RALPH (*bitterly*) No, you bring us up in the image of what *you think* we should be. What *you want* us to be. Then you despise us for actually being it!

BEL I told you, he should be telling all this to his mother.

RALPH (*violently*) Christ, there's nothing special about you. There's nothing mysterious. You're just a wreck on the highway! I wouldn't touch you, and even if I did, I wouldn't, and even if you want me to, I won't. I mean, the only woman that interests me is the one who deals straight off the top of the pack. I'm just a guy, can't you understand? I'm just a man. Take it or leave it. I'm nothing special. So don't expect it from me. GET IT!

(RALPH *storms into the bathroom.* A MAN *knocks violently at the door.*)

MAN (OFF) Taissez vous! J'en mar! (*Pause, more knocking*) Vous êtes fou? Vous savez l'heure, eh? (*Silence.* LOUISE *goes to the door and opens it a little. The man has gone. She goes into the corridor. She enters closing the door.*)

LOUISE I think someone was trying to get to sleep. Huh.

BEL (*longingly*) Oh, sleep. (*Yawns*) I'd love to go to sleep. I'm so tired. Aren't you tired?

LOUISE What do you think?

(LOUISE *goes out on to the balcony. The toilet flushes.* RALPH *enters and slumps into a chair.*)

BEL (*reflectively*) My father used to spend hours in the bathroom. He used to go in there with his papers and his king-sized cigarettes. When he'd finished you had to cut your way in through the fog. As he got older, he used to pee on the floor. It still amazes me that he couldn't direct it into the bowl. Of course, my mother cleaned up. Mopped up after him. Her face in the bowl. I used to rush in and draw the curtains and open the window. Let in the light. Let in the fresh air. Let out the fog. (*Brief pause*) What made me remember that? (*Yawns.*) It's like a dream now. A thing of the past.

LOUISE (*matter of fact*) I had a dream last night.

BEL Good was it?

LOUISE I wrote it down. It was just a flood of images. Words. When I woke, I wrote it down.

BEL I love dreams.

LOUISE Do you? Do you want me to read it?

RALPH Oh, God.

BEL (*looking at* RALPH) Yes. Why not. You read it.

LOUISE Okay.

(LOUISE *collects the piece of paper from her bag and sits on the bed.*)

(*reading, fluently, without embellishment*) Grey, all uncompromising skies, all through, everywhere, within and without, on the pavement, behind the tree, nothing untouched, broken hearts at every corner, even the small child on the roundabout, eyeless and dirty, the windows in the town are smashed, a circle of misery, never ending, forever, unless the eyeless child is taken and comforted.

(*Pause.*)

BEL That's a dream?

LOUISE Yes.

BEL What does it mean?

LOUISE I can't tell you. I know, but I can't say why.

RALPH Who the hell's the eyeless child?

(*Pause.*)

BEL (*yawns*) It's too late to think. I'm too tired. I can't take it. I need my eight hours.

LOUISE Yes, it's late. You sleep.

BEL You don't mind? You don't mind me sleeping here?

LOUISE It's OK, you sleep. We'll try and keep it quiet.

BEL Oh, thanks. Thank you.

(BEL *switches off the lights around the bed. She undresses down to her briefs.* LOUISE *looks at* RALPH. RALPH *looks away.* BEL *gets into bed.*)

(*yawns*) Oh, this is lovely. Mmmnn. Goodnight.

(LOUISE *switches off the remaining lights except those close to* RALPH. *She goes back to the bed and turns back the bed clothes leaving* BEL *covered by a sheet.)*

Mmmnn. Thanks.

LOUISE Goodnight Bel.

(*Pause.*)

(LOUISE *pours a drink. After a time she sits close to* RALPH.)

RALPH Well?

LOUISE I've always dealt off the top.

RALPH Oh yes?

LOUISE You know I have.

RALPH So?

LOUISE So.

RALPH I think you ought to explain yourself.

LOUISE Why?

RALPH Why!

LOUISE Ssh, she's trying to sleep.

RALPH What do I care.

LOUISE (*bitterly*) I thought you were a man of the world. I thought you were much bigger than the show I've witnessed tonight.

RALPH (*decisively*) If you cheat on me, I go cold. I freeze over. That's the way it is with me.

LOUISE What do you mean, cheat? Cheat? What's that?

RALPH It's cheat. I understand the word quite easily.

LOUISE So what do you call this? What's this if it's not cheating? You think I'm not *deeply hurt* by this?

RALPH This is nothing. You know that. This is just pathetic revenge. Yours wasn't. You took a lover.

LOUISE I did not!

RALPH (*passionately*) I'm your lover.

(*Pause.*)

Oh, I can't cope with all this kind of talk. I just feel like I'm stupid. So she has a lover. OK. That's OK. I can cope with that. What am I going on about? It's not as if it's important.

LOUISE (*precisely*) I did not take a lover. I've never loved anyone, except you. (*Brief pause*) You're just using it as an excuse. Don't you know?

RALPH No, I don't know. I don't know the answers to the questions. I don't think I even know the questions anymore. I'm in the dark these days.

LOUISE You think I'm not in the dark?

RALPH (*disbelief*) You?

LOUISE Day by day, for as many days as possible. That's what we agreed. Until the days run out. We just stopped being vigilant.

RALPH No, it was fine until this 'Other Life' started up.

LOUISE You think I've got it together, don't you? My God, that's so far from the truth.

RALPH (*coldly*) What truth?

LOUISE Well, I would like to tell the truth, I would, if I knew the truth. My truth. But I've no idea. I reconstruct myself each day. (*Longingly*) If I had the *guts*, I'd stay that person, you know, that person, at that moment between sleep and being awake. That person. Who just. . .*IS*. Without a past. Without a future. A person who's happy just looking at the light. (*Pause*) I mean, as soon as I'm awake, as soon as I think I know who I am, I go through the farce. I have a coffee, a cigarette, make phone calls. . .

RALPH Attend meetings.

LOUISE OK. OK! I'm driven. By what, I don't know. I also need attention. Your attention. I do. I'm not holding anything back, Ralph. I mean, I'd listen to anyone to keep from being on my own.

RALPH (*shocked*) What?

LOUISE The great thing is not to stop. If I stopped now, I think I'd collapse. You see, you musn't think I think very highly of myself. I'm not superior. (*Laughs*) I constantly think, people think very little of me.

(*Brief pause.*)

RALPH But you are a success. You have success.

LOUISE Does that bother you?

RALPH No.

LOUISE Are you sure?

RALPH I wanted you to work. I just didn't think it would change you.

LOUISE Well, if I have changed, it's because it's hard. It's still a man's world you know, and every man I meet still tries to dominate me.

RALPH (*hesitates*) But you appear so confident.

LOUISE I have no other choice.

(*Silence.*)

(RALPH *takes* LOUISE's *glass and drinks. He hands it back.*)

RALPH (*grudgingly*) I do like your hair.

LOUISE You do?

RALPH She's right. It's neat. It makes you look younger.

LOUISE I know.

(*Pause.*)

RALPH I remember you.

(*Pause.*)

I remember Hammersmith. Yogurt for breakfast.

(*Pause.*)

You were mad for rhubarb yogurt.

LOUISE I was pregnant.

RALPH Rhubarb yogurt for breakfast in that green kitchen. And that album.

LOUISE What album?

RALPH Nashville Skyline. Dylan.

LOUISE Nashville Skyline?

RALPH We used to play it all the time. And after the yogurt. . .there were fresh warm rolls. . .and boiled eggs.

LOUISE (*hesitates, anguished*) Oh. . .that's what the tray was about.

(*Pause.*)

RALPH My God, it's so *bland* nowadays! I mean, that place in Hammersmith, those records. They were banging on the wall all hours. And when I first met you. A basement. It was a basement party in Belsize Park. You were in a hideously bright kaftan and I was draped in some Mexican blanket!

LOUISE You were also barefoot.

RALPH Oh no I wasn't. I was far too wary of the dog shit to go barefoot.

(*Pause.*)

Hell, you look good to me.

LOUISE So do you. You look better than ever.

(*Pause.*)

RALPH Huh. How could you forget Nashville Skyline?

LOUISE I don't know.

RALPH But how could you? I remember it vividly. I went out in the *rain* to get that album. I went up the Goldhawk Road in the rain to that record exchange. I gave them your Buffy Saint Marie, they gave me Bob Dylan. I can remember the cars. I waded through polluted air for that album. And we played it all night. You lay on the bed. On that quilt. That red patchwork quilt. How can you forget?

LOUISE It must have slipped my mind.

RALPH (*shocked*) But we played that album to our friends. We bored the arses off our friends playing that album.

LOUISE (*tentatively*) Well. To tell you the truth. I never really liked Nashville Skyline.

RALPH (*brief pause*) What?

LOUISE I never liked it.

RALPH I don't believe you.

LOUISE I've never liked Country and Western.

RALPH Yes, but it wasn't real Country and Western.

LOUISE Well, it sounded like it to me.

RALPH (*brief pause*) I don't believe this. You didn't like it?

LOUISE Along with our friends, it bored the arse off me.

RALPH (*amazed*) How can you say that?

LOUISE (*hesitates*) But surely you knew?

RALPH Knew? Of course I didn't know.

LOUISE Oh, I thought you knew. You see, I thought you only played it to annoy me.

RALPH *What?* Why the hell would I do that?

LOUISE (*matter of fact*) Because I didn't like it.

RALPH But I only played it because *you* liked it.

LOUISE (*wary*) Oh, no. That's not true.

RALPH Yes, it is Louise. You know it is.

LOUISE Oh no, no, you only played it because *you* liked it. Come on Ralph, you know that's the truth.

(*Brief pause.*)

RALPH Well. Well, if you really want the truth. . .I didn't like it either.

(*Brief pause.*)

LOUISE *You didn't?*

RALPH No.

LOUISE Oh come on, you loved it.

RALPH No I didn't.

LOUISE What do you mean?

RALPH Well, I wasn't really that taken with it.

LOUISE I don't believe you.

RALPH It's true. I'm telling the truth. I've always loathed Country and Western.

LOUISE (*indignantly*) Then *why* in God's name did you play it?

RALPH I played it because *you* liked it! I only liked the albums he made before the crash. You know, before he had that crash.

LOUISE Then why didn't you play those albums? The albums before the crash.

RALPH I didn't play them Louise, because I thought you didn't like the albums he made before the crash.

LOUISE Well I didn't.

RALPH I thought so.

LOUISE I didn't like any of his albums. I couldn't make out a word he was singing.

RALPH (*shocked*) What are you talking about? The words are perfectly clear. They're great words. Poems. *They're as clear as day*.

LOUISE (*emphatically*) Not to me.

(*Pause.*)

RALPH (*persistent, without embellishment*) I asked, would you like his new album? You replied, yes. I asked, are you sure? Are you really sure? I mean, it's really chucking it down outside. It's really foul outside. Do you really want it? And you answered, *Yes*.

LOUISE (*defiantly*) I lied.

RALPH Lied?

LOUISE Yes.

RALPH Well, fuck me!

LOUISE (*quickly*) I thought you wanted the album, and I thought you wanted me to want the album, because if I wanted the album, you could buy it, and not feel guilty about wanting it for yourself, and therefore not feel guilty about imposing what you wanted on me.

(*Pause.*)

RALPH My God, I wish I'd known that before!

(*Blackout*)

ACT TWO

Sunrise

LOUISE *is in the bathroom.*

RALPH *is slumped in an armchair.*

BEL *is asleep on the bed.*

(*Silence.*)

LOUISE My God, I look terrible.

(LOUISE *enters from the bathroom drying her neck and hands. She pauses to listen to distant voices in the hotel. She looks at* RALPH.)

LOUISE I knew you'd come here, Ralph. It's not in your nature to try out a new place.

RALPH Huh.

(LOUISE *goes to the dressing table and gets her make-up out of her bag. She switches on a small light.*)

LOUISE (*cleaning her face*) It all started here, didn't it? It all started that day we went into that record shop on the Rue. . .anyway that was the day. Do you remember those two guys, with their afro hair and their crocodile boots? I asked about some record and they said, Is this Rock and Rock? I wanted them to play the first track. I wanted to hear it. But you threw a minor fit and started muttering, muttering something like, Oh they wouldn't know Rock and Rock if it sat on their face. You dragged me out that shop, and we didn't speak till we'd climbed up the Rue Descartes to the Place de la Contrescarpe. Oh yes, I remember all of it. The heat that summer, worse than this summer. It was a Saturday, and then you started going on about, how Spurs were playing the Gunners at White Hart Lane. How Chivers was playing, and you were in Paris with me.

RALPH Huh.

LOUISE Then we entered a really seedy cafe in the square, and ordered two coffees, and you made me smoke my first

Gitane. I choked myself silly. (*Brief pause*) Then you took a ring from your pocket and placed it on the third finger of my left hand.

(*Pause.*)

And that night, in a room here . . . the constant movement and noise on the stairs . . . and we lay on that small bed and rolled into the centre and stuck to each other in the heat.

(*Pause.*)

Oh yes, It was the deepest sleep of my life.

(*Pause.*)

Look at my face.

(LOUISE *inspects her face. She starts to make up.*)

(*reflectively*) I haven't done an all-nighter for years. (*Brief pause*) My first big all-nighter was with you. Did you know? That was when you took me up to Parliament Hill Fields to hear the Pink Floyd. We came over the crest of the hill, and there they were, in the bowl, with the crowd, playing 'Be Careful with that Axe, Eugene'. The sound floated on the night air. And then you gave me my first *joint.* (*She checks her watch*) I must make some phone calls today.

(*Pause.*)

We were walking back afterwards. (*She hesitates*) We were walking down a street. There was this *shape* in the middle of the street. It looked bad. It looked really bad. It felt bad. It seemed to rear up and get bigger. It seemed to swallow up the street. And then it came towards us. I held your hand. It had eyes. I was terrified. I remember thinking I was going to die, and that I'd never take dope ever again. And then, as we passed it, I looked. And all I saw . . . was just a piece of dirty rag twitching in the breeze. (*Brief pause*) I said, that's a relief. And you, you said, yes.

(*Pause.*)

(*realization*) That was enough for me. To know that. You can't get any closer.

(*Pause.* LOUISE *shudders and takes out her filofax and pen.*)

I must call Jane before she leaves for New York. And Susan, no she doesn't get back till Tuesday.

(*writing*) Jenny.

(LOUISE *puts the filofax back in her bag and completes her make-up.*)

No, there isn't anything else except *that.* But we have to go forward. There's no way back. There's nothing back there for us. Just memories. Of course, if we flew back today, I could get some work done. I'd be ahead. I could get Jordan to come in with me. We could lunch together. Have you seen her art work lately? My God, has that girl got talent. And she's so sharp, she won't take it from anyone. I admire that. (*Looking at* BEL) They're going to be some generation when they crack it. I mean, they're cracking it already. Those girls won't take it from anyone.

(LOUISE *switches off the light. She sits back and stares at the sunrise.*)

Isn't that beautiful. It makes me shiver.

(LOUISE *goes out on to the balcony. She stretches, leans against the door frame.*)

(*quickly, without pausing*) No, the thing is, Ralph, I can't start up again with someone else. I haven't got the energy. I can't go through all those excited conversations again. You know, all those family stories. I did this, then I did that stuff. All that getting to know one another. I can't face that again. Once is enough for anyone. Anyway where would I find the time?

(*Pause.*)

(*tenderly*) No. I like coming home to you. *I know you.* I like to know you're there. It makes me feel good to know you're there. (*Brief pause*) It really shook me when you weren't. It really disturbed me. (*Brief pause*) Yes, let's forget all this and go home. It's a *new* day. It's going to be another hot day. A good day. I bet someone gets lucky out there today, and why shouldn't it be us? (LOUISE *comes back into the room.*) So? What do you think? What do you say? Let's go home. Let's forget all this and go back today. Ralph? Ralph? Ralph?

RALPH Mmmnnn...

LOUISE Are you asleep?

RALPH Eh?

LOUISE (*hurt*) You've been asleep. I thought you just had your eyes shut. You've been asleep.

RALPH (*startled*) What? What? What is it? What's up?

LOUISE You've been asleep.

RALPH What! I'm still in Paris, am I? What's been happening here? Oh God...

(*Slight pause.*)

LOUISE I thought you were listening to me.

RALPH (*leaping up quickly*) We're all still here, are we? We're all still here where we left off. Christ, my head. What time is it?

LOUISE It's nearly six.

RALPH Six? Six o'clock? In the morning?

LOUISE (*subdued*) I'll get you a glass of water.

(LOUISE *exits into the bathroom.*)

RALPH (*yawns and stretches*) So. We're all still here. Huh. I thought we'd gone. It must have been a dream.

LOUISE (*entering*) Your water.

RALPH (*drinks*) I hate water.

(*Pause.*)

LOUISE Let's go home Ralph. Let's go home today.

RALPH What?

LOUISE Let's go home *together*.

RALPH (*brief pause*) Why?

LOUISE Why? Why do you think?

RALPH (*coldly*) Got some work to do, have you?

LOUISE No, it's Sunday today. If we can get an early plane we'd be back in time to read the papers in the garden. We could go to the Chequers for lunch. What do you think? (*Brief pause*) Of course, if you'd rather be on your own, I can always take Jordan to the office and put in a few hours.

RALPH A few hours.

LOUISE You know it's good fun at the Chequers. There's always a great crowd there on a Sunday. We could have a few drinks.

RALPH I don't want to be hanging around waiting for you. That's not my idea of a Sunday afternoon.

LOUISE Oh, please come. I want you to come. So does Jordan.

RALPH Why can't Jordan come here? We could show her Paris. Why don't we all stay here for a week? I haven't got a concert to cover for a week. There's things I want to see here. There's that Matisse exhibition. We could have a good time. We could do a bit of walking. (*Brief pause*) Why can't we do what *I* want to do? You know I love you, Louise. Why can't you do it for me?

LOUISE (*hesitates*) Please come home, Ralph.

(BEL *wakes up, yawns and stretches. She sits up and pulls on her T-shirt.*)

BEL Good morning everyone.

(BEL *gets out of bed and smiles at* RALPH *and* LOUISE. *She goes to the bathroom.*)

LOUISE (*suddenly exploding*) Oh, for God's sake Ralph, are you coming back or not!

RALPH (*brief pause, coldly*) No. I'm staying in Paris.

LOUISE (*despairingly*) You know I can't stay. You think just because I'm a woman I can walk out on my job. You're doing this on purpose.

RALPH (*calmly*) I can't remember the last time you did something for me.

LOUISE I could say the same about you. Oh Ralph, it's been far too many years for us not to go on with it. We just can't let everything go and *hang out* here.

RALPH Why not?

LOUISE Why not? Because we have to get on.

RALPH (*derisively*) Get on? Get on? Get on to *where*?

LOUISE (*precisely*) If it was you who had to work tomorrow you'd expect me to come. You wouldn't give it a moment's thought.

RALPH (*expansively*) But if you stay with me, we could have lunch in the open. That's better than the Chequers. That's better than rubbing shoulders with that crowd of Fascists. You could have Moules. You know how you like Moules. I'll let you finish the bread, so you can mop up all the sauce.

LOUISE Oh Ralph, you can get Moules anywhere these days.

(*Pause. The toilet flushes.* BEL *enters brushing her teeth and goes to the balcony.*)

BEL (*optimistically*) Well, it certainly looks like it's going to be another great day. We should go to the coast. A day on the beach. We'd all feel better for a little beach life. (*To* RALPH) What do you think?

RALPH What do *I* think? I think Louise is going back to England today.

BEL (*saddened*) Oh.

RALPH It doesn't matter what I say. She'll do exactly what she wants to do. That is 'How It Is' I'm afraid. (*To* LOUISE) Whatever I say will have no bearing on the outcome.

BEL (*innocently*) But what about us?

RALPH Us?

BEL What's the plan? Is there a plan? Where shall we go? You know, visits, excursions. I mean, we've got to go somewhere. We can't stay here all day. We'd be crawling up the wall if we stay here. I mean, I know it's a good laugh.

RALPH (*abruptly*) What's a good laugh?

BEL (*hesitates*) Last night. I thought it was a bit of a hoot.

RALPH A what?

BEL A hoot.

RALPH A hoot!

BEL Well, I think a day out would do us good. I think we'd all benefit from an outing.

RALPH (*vehemently*) I don't give a fuck what you think!

(RALPH *exits into the bathroom. Pause.*)

BEL (*aggressively, loud*) Well, I happen to like Nashville Skyline.

(*Pause.* RALPH *enters.*)

RALPH (*calmly*) What did you say?

BEL (*hesitates*) Well, I know it was before my time, but I quite like it. It's...

RALPH (*abruptly*) It's what?

BEL It's romantic. But that's OK. I like a little romance. (*Brief pause*) Of course that's the trouble. You were all too romantic. You loved all that, didn't you? All your lot. You know, 'All You Need Is Love'. Except... You thought sex was love and love was sex. (*Brief pause*) It's quite touching really...if you forget to laugh.

(*Silence.*)

I think we should get them to send up a plateful of croissants.

LOUISE It's too early. Everyone is still asleep.

BEL Asleep? Who's been asleep? No one sleeps round you two except the dead.

(*Silence.*)

RALPH (*bitterly*) We should have never left the city. We should have stayed in the city. We should have stayed in Hammersmith. We should have never have left that green kitchen.

LOUISE Oh God.

RALPH It's true.

LOUISE But it was so small. I couldn't turn round in it. *You* forget. Anyway I hated the colour. Olive green.

RALPH It wasn't olive green.

LOUISE (*aggressively*) Oh yes? Well, what was it if it wasn't olive green? Come on Ralph, you're the one who could see. You remember? *The light*.

RALPH (*hesitates*) It was just green. Green.

LOUISE (*patronizingly*) It was in that kitchen that you said to me. . . that you'd seen light falling on light.

BEL What? Light falling on light?

LOUISE Yes.

BEL What's that?

LOUISE It's light falling on light. (*Brief pause*) Oh, I was so impressed. I had never seen it. Light on light. I thought it made you special. A special person. You had seen. You knew. You had been there. It made me doubt myself. You see, I had never seen or experienced anything so extraordinary. I was just ordinary. It made me feel ordinary. *You* made me feel ordinary. But I'm not ordinary, am I? I mean, anyone can see light, if they care to look, and if they have enough time, and take enough *drugs*!

(RALPH *leaps up and starts packing his case.*)

(*wearily*) I can't say goodbye again, Ralph.

RALPH (*violently*) Who do you think you are? Coming in here in your designer clothes with your make-up and your missionary mouth. I tell you, you can erase where I've been, and what I've seen, and you can count your credit cards, but you can't touch me!

(RALPH *exits into the bathroom. Pause.*)

BEL I'm sorry I set him off. (*Brief pause*) I have to have something to look forward to when I wake up. I can't bear it if I've nothing to do. (*Brief pause*) I'm sorry.

LOUISE It's not your fault.

BEL (*hestitates*) I don't suppose you'd like to go to Florence?

LOUISE Oh I'm sure you'll find someone. You'll be happy.

BEL I hate travelling alone. (*Brief pause*) Anyway, I think it's difficult to be happy these days. Happiness feels false.

(*Pause.* RALPH *enters. He throws his washing kit into his case.*)

RALPH Well, that's that.

LOUISE So where are you going this time?

RALPH Where am I going?

LOUISE Yes, I'd like to know, thank you. What are you going to do?

RALPH I'll tell you. I'll tell you what *I* think. I was fencing one morning.

LOUISE Fencing?

RALPH Yes, and I pulled a hamstring. It was a really bad pain. I had to hobble home. Well, I put my leg up, but after a while the pain was still quite intense, so I decided to take some Acid. To see if it might ease the pain. I had a few tabs. A friend of mine had sent me some, lodged in the spine of his copy of the Koran. . .and so that afternoon I took some. (*Brief pause*) Well, after about twenty minutes, I must have forgotten, because I took some more. And then, God knows why, about a quarter of an hour later, I took a little bit more. 'Set The Controls For The Heart Of The Sun' was on the turntable. Then I blacked out. (*Brief pause*) Complete darkness. I have no memory of what the blackout was like. It was empty, I suppose. (*Brief pause*) Well, when I came to, I found myself lying face down on the bed. It was dark. The air was full of sound. Of noises. Clicking noises. Noises in the wall. In the skirting boards. Moving, colour noises. It was only later I realized it was the needle. The record hadn't turned itself off. (*Brief pause*) Well, somehow, I got to my feet, and found myself facing myself in the mirror. Of course I didn't know it was me. I didn't recognize my face. It was moving you see. It was constantly changing shape. Sometimes it was my mother's face, sometimes my father's. I know that now, but then I didn't know. (*Brief pause*) I was truly terrified. Intense, painful, terror. I did not know my name. I couldn't find it in any part of me. I was nameless. (*Pause*) So. I stood there...without a name...and then I heard a voice. The voice said, 'You are on a planet. You are on a planet spinning through space'. Well, as you can imagine, anyone whose having difficulty remembering his name is bound to be fucked by that one. A planet? What's a planet? I didn't know. It was as if everything had been erased from my mind. You see, I had to start again, from the beginning, building myself. Block by block. (*Pause*) Well, gradually...it was hours, but it felt like weeks, and well, I managed to pull myself back in from out there. You know, back in from the void. And well, I was finally in some kind of shape where it was possible to say...I was Ralph. (*Brief pause*) It was then, and it was only then, that it really started. Who was Ralph? Where did he come from? What did he do? And why did he do it? Occasionally I seemed to hit a truth, and my stomach would shudder each time I accepted the truth. Truths about myself. About my nature. Oh, some of them were very little truths...like admitting my mother actually loved my father more than she loved me. A wretched truth if you've believed otherwise. A truth that casts you adrift. Or the reason I couldn't live without a woman. . . I couldn't live without a woman because I was still in need of the love I'd never had. (*Brief pause*) These *small* openings were accompanied by tears, immense feelings, immense sadness. . . but I was alive, and I knew I was alive. It was 1968 and I knew I was here. (*Pause*) Of course, it's impossible to continue in that state. No one can or wishes to live in a state of compassion for one's self. . . or others. (*Brief pause*) So gradually it went away. The doors closed. The hardness came back. And I stopped seeing. . . trees. . . old people. . . babies' faces. I stopped seeing it all. . . until it was just me again. (*Brief pause*) Me. With my little problems. My this. My that. (*Bitterly*) I mean, I don't even see clouds anymore. I just get annoyed when they block out the sun. (*Pause*) Give us a cigarette.

(LOUISE *gives* RALPH *a cigarette and lights it for him.* RALPH *coughs. Pause.*)

LOUISE (*conciliatory*) We could always move. We could move back to London.

RALPH Where in London?

LOUISE I don't know. Highgate?

RALPH I hate Highgate.

LOUISE What about Belsize Park?

RALPH I'm known in Belsize Park.

LOUISE Well, all I'm saying is we can move back if you want.

BEL I used to live in Wandsworth. Do you know Wandsworth?

LOUISE Well yes, I suppose we could even go south of the river. I'm even prepared to do that.

RALPH (*decisively*) *NO*. You've got your work. You've got your daughter. You don't need me. Anyway I can't supply what you need. But don't you worry, you can get a door mat anywhere. I mean, I'm very grateful, but you stick with your magazine. With your deodorants and autumn fashions and face creams. OK? I'm sure that'll keep you warm in the winter.

LOUISE (*coldly*) I started again from the bottom, and I made it. I cracked it. Against all the odds. What do you want me to do? Give it away?

RALPH My money helped you.

LOUISE Sure. I can't thank you enough. But I love it. I love the magazine and I love to work.

RALPH Oh yes, we all love the magazine. We all love the feel of the paper. It's so smooth. So cool. (*Vehemently*) And so full of *nothing*!

LOUISE (*violently*) You bastard! I came here. I needn't have come.

RALPH So what.

LOUISE So it shows. It shows!

RALPH What does it show?

LOUISE It shows I'm prepared to listen to you. To take a considerable amount of abuse. I mean, I didn't need to listen. I didn't need to listen to any of it.

RALPH And you didn't, did you? In fact, you've forgotten how to listen.

LOUISE (*exploding*) All right! All right! I want it all! Don't you turn your face away from me! You listen to me. I want it all! Work. Jordan. You. And I don't see why I have to ask for it. It's mine by right. Why should I have to ask for it? How dare you try and make me feel guilty for wanting it. I'm not doing anything abnormal. My God, you've got a bloody nerve! Christ! I've been listening to *CRAP FROM MEN* for years and years and *YEARS*! Your self-pitying whine *DEAFENS ME*!

(RALPH *walks straight out on to the balcony*.)

You can't take it, can you?

RALPH (*entering, calmly*) Who? Me?

LOUISE Oh, you pretend. Lip service. You make noises. We must let them have their heads. You know, for a short while. Let them sound off. Oh yes. But really, you *hate* it. You really believe I've stepped way over the line!

RALPH (*nonchalantly*) Are you by any chance talking to me? Is that what you are doing? You know me, do you?

LOUISE It's eating you alive I'm having a good time. It wrecks you I function out there. I mean, I don't need to be held up anymore. (*Triumphantly*) I'm good! I'm really *good*! And you hate it so much, you actually want to go back to the old ways. The good old days. You want me back under the thumb where you can keep an eye on me. Well, I tell you I'm *not* going back. I'm *never* going back. *NEVER*!

RALPH (*extraordinary violence*) Christ! You must be in the wrong cinema. This is cinema two. What one do you want? Cinema one? Oh, cinema one. . .well, that's out the door, along the corridor, down the stairs. . .*AND ACROSS THE FUCKING STREET*!

(*Brief pause.*)

LOUISE (*precise*) Right in your centre, right down there. . .there's a part of you that will never change. It's that part that cannot come to terms with what's happened to me. I mean, how can you allow *a mere woman* to talk to you like this. How dare she raise her voice. How dare she call the shots. How dare she have any opinions about anything! I mean, who the hell does she think she is? *A HUMAN BEING*!

RALPH (*ice*) It's OK, Louise. It's OK. I've told you. I've finished with it. I've jacked it. The next time you want a session, forget it. If you want it that bad, you'll have to go out and pay for it.

LOUISE (*wearily*) Is that all you have to say?

RALPH (*ice*) When you've got a day off work, when you've got an *hour*. . .you can buy me lunch. OK?

(*A* MAN *knocks violently at the door.*)

MAN (OFF) (*violently*) Merde Alors! Taissez vous! Taissez vous! Vous savez l'heure! Les Anglais. . . Shit!

RALPH Oh, piss off!

(*A disturbed muttering outside the door. Silence.*)

LOUISE (*abruptly, to* BEL) Well, you were right.

BEL Me? Right? What about?

LOUISE Oh, you were just right.

BEL What did I say that was right?

LOUISE You have to take it as you see it, not as you want it to be.

BEL I know.

LOUISE (*brief pause, to* RALPH) It's clear, if you can't change, I can't help you. It has to come from you.

RALPH Oh, I'll change all right. But it won't be the way you want. The way you need. You've made your bed, you lie in it.

LOUISE (*briskly*) Sure. OK. Fine. (*She collects her bag. Abruptly, to* BEL) So what do you say to breakfast?

BEL Me?

LOUISE Yes. You.

BEL Oh, I'd lovc it.

RALPH You're not. . . huh. . . you're not going with her.

LOUISE Well, get your things together and I'll buy you breakfast.

RALPH (*brief pause*) I don't believe it.

(BEL *rushes into the bathroom to collect her wash bag.*)

LOUISE (*calls*) Where shall we go?

BEL Oh let's go up to the Place du Tertre. I love it up there. Do you want a big breakfast or just coffee and croissants?

RALPH You're not really going...you can't go with her.

LOUISE (*overlapping, defiantly*) Oh, I feel like a big breakfast this morning!

(BEL *enters.*)

BEL Yes, so do I. I'm absolutely starved.

RALPH Christ.

(BEL *collects her things and puts them into her shoulder bag. She checks her hair in the mirror.*)

BEL I was going to ask you. What do you think? Do you think I should get my hair cut?

LOUISE Why not, if you fancy a change.

BEL Well, I thought I'd try it short too. Do you think I'd look good with short hair?

RALPH Oh, why don't you go all the way and shave your head. Then you wouldn't have a single thing to think about!

(*Silence.* BEL *exits.*)

LOUISE Well, goodbye Ralph.

RALPH (*anguished*) How the hell do you and I go forward from here? How do we go forward? (*Brief pause*) *HOW*?

LOUISE Oh come on Ralph, one big step, and the rest's easy. After all it's only Rock and Roll.

RALPH Rock and Roll?

LOUISE Yes.

RALPH (*emphatically*) No, Rock and Roll's dead.

(*Pause.* LOUISE *exits.*)

(*to himself after a pause*) It died years ago.

(*Blackout.*)

PROPERTY LIST

Furniture

Bed
Dressing table, chair
2 armchairs
Small table
Wardrobe

Act One, Scene One

On Stage

Suitcase
Newspapers
Magazines
Cassette recorder
Cassette tapes
Wine bottles (empty)
Wine bottle (¾ full)
2 wine glasses
Condoms (BEL)

Off Stage

Satchel (LOUISE) including:
filofax
cigarettes
make-up
various papers, pens

Empty glass (RALPH)
Wine bottle (full)

Act One, Scene Two

On Stage

Wine bottle (¼ full)

Act Two

Off Stage

Hand towel (LOUISE)
Toothbrush (BEL)
Washing kit (RALPH)
Washing kit (BEL)

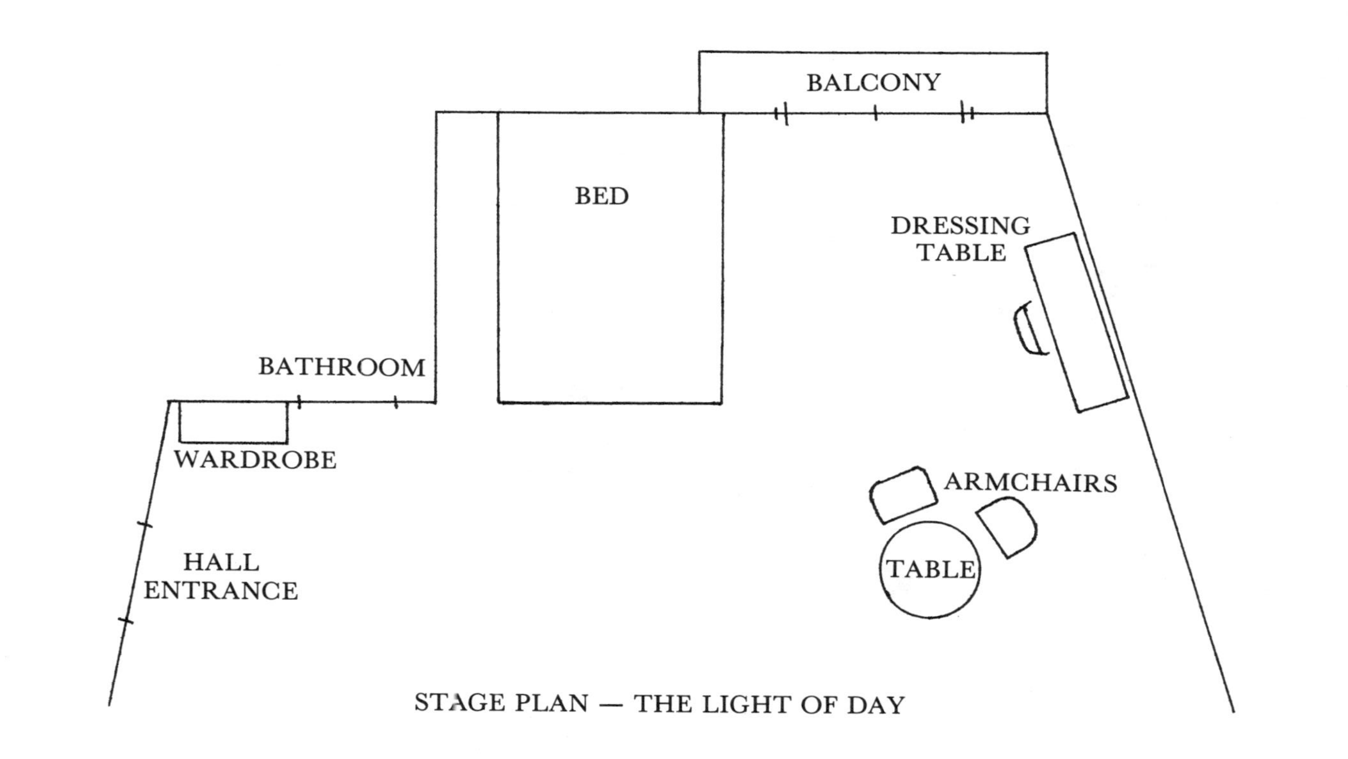

STAGE PLAN — THE LIGHT OF DAY

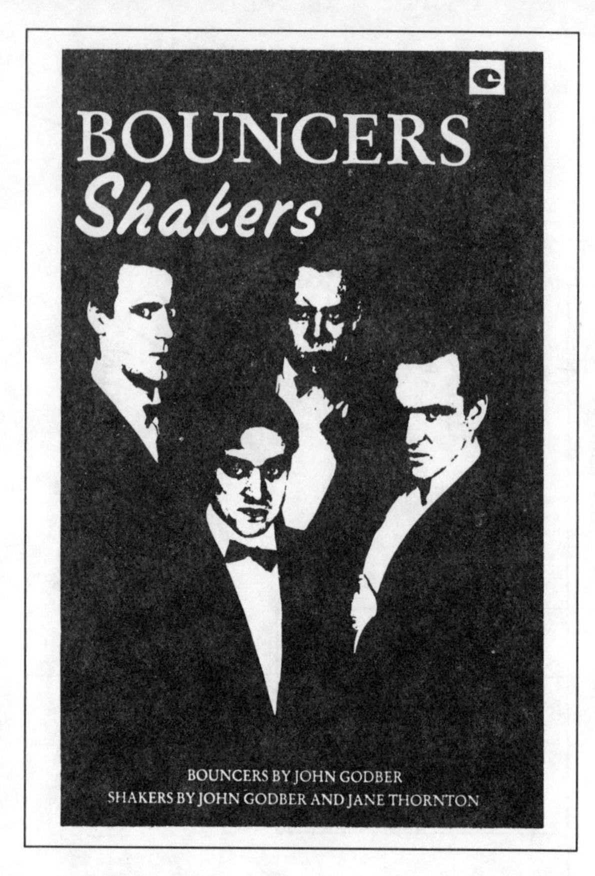

Bouncers and *Shakers*, a volume of two plays, now available from Chappell Plays.

It's Friday night, it's disco night — time for 'Bouncers' to come alive! In this outrageous and hilarious parody of the contemporary disco scene, four brutish bouncers portraying over twenty different characters invite us for a night out on the town. Join them on the disco floor where the pulsating beat and flashing lights mesmerize the groovers. 'Brilliant . . . consistently entertaining' *Evening Standard*.

Shakers is the local trendy cocktail bar where everyone wants to be seen: from the check-out girls to the chinless wonders, the yuppies to the local lads tittering at the thought of a 'Long Slow Comfortable Screw'. We are given a wickedly funny glimpse of this world by four waitresses who offer a fascinating view of the reality that lurks behind the plastic palms and Pina Coladas.

For further information, contact Chappell Plays Ltd, 129 Park Street, London W1Y 3FA. Telephone 01-629 7600.

MUMBO JUMBO

ROBIN GLENDINNING

Set in a Protestant boy's public school in present-day Belfast, this both humorous and touching play centres on the sexual discovery and political awakening of two classmates, the poetic and idealistic Dunham, and his fiercely Orange friend, Creaney. School is seen as a world which both reflects and reinforces the rigid tribalism and sectarianism of Ulster politics. The schoolboys' chant of Vachel Lindsay's menacingly rhythmic poem, *The Congo*, acts as a powerful central metaphor, weaving its way relentlessly through the action of the play as it mesmerizes the innocent young minds.

Mumbo Jumbo was joint winner of the 1985 Mobil Playwriting Competition.

'Robin Glendinning... one of our most interesting new arrivals. An original and buccaneering sensibility, full of dark humour and fearless common sense... a play of intellectual ferocity.' *Sunday Times.*

For further information, contact Chappell Plays Ltd, 129 Park Street, London W1Y 3FA. Telephone 01-629 7600.